L'universe Knows That
You Are The Best
I0791280

Cover design by Ruby Huang (HsiaoHan)
Illustrated by Ruby Huang (HsiaoHan)
Editted by Samuel Ho (Cheuk Wai)
Typography: Samuel Ho (Cheuk Wai)

Toronto, Ontario, Canada

If you're bored, visit us on:

Facebook

https://www.facebook.com/LuniverseStories

or

Instagram

@luniverse_stories

# For YOU

I've learned that
people will forget what you said,
people will forget what you did,
but people will never forget
HOW YOU MADE THEM FEEL.

– Maya Angelou
(Author)

The secret of
SUCCESS
is to do the common thing
uncommonly well.

- John D. Rockefeller Jr.
(Philanthropist)

Don't be distracted by criticism.
REMEMBER!
The only taste of success some people get
is to take a bite out of you.

- Zig Ziglar
(Author)

Go CONFIDENTLY
in the direction of your dream!
Live the life you've imagined.

- Henry David Thoreau
(Philosopher)

If you are not willing to RISK the usual,
you will have to SETTLE for the ordinary.
— Jim Rohn
(Author)

Believe you can
and you're halfway there.
- Theodore Roosevelt
(25th president of the United States)

NEVER LET
the fear of striking out
keep you from
playing the game.
- Babe Ruth
(Baseball Superstar)

You have brains in your brain.
You have feet in your shoes.
You can steer yourself
any direction you choose.

- Dr. Seuss
(Author)

Whatever the mind of man
can conceive and believe.

It can achieve.
- Napoleon Hill
(Author)

I would rather
DIE OF PASSION
than of boredom.
- Vincent Van Gogh
(Artist)

In the end, it's not
the years in your life that count.

It's the life in your years.
-Abraham Lincoln
(16th President of the United States)

Always remember that you are absolutely UNIQUE.
Just like everyone else.

-Margaret Mead
(Anthropologist)

**"I've learned that people will forget what you said,
people will forget what you did,
but people will never forget how you made them feel."**
*-Maya Angelou*
*American author, actress, and civil rights activist
who was famous for her autobiographies, poetry and essays.*

**"The secret of success
is to do the common thing uncommonly well."**
*-John D. Rockefeller Jr.*
*American financier and philanthropist who advocated
for better industrial working conditions after World War I.*

**"Don't be distracted by criticism.
Remember -- the only taste of success some people get
is to take a bite out of you."**
*-Zig Ziglar*
*American author, salesman, and motivational speaker.*

**"Go confidently in the direction of your dreams!
Live the life you've imagined."**
*-Henry David Thoreau*
*American essayist, poet and philosopher
who was best known for his book Walden.*

**"If you are not willing to risk the usual,
you will have to settle for the ordinary."**
*-Jim Rohn*
*American entrepreneur, author and motivational speaker.*

**"Believe you can and you're halfway there."**
*-Theodore Roosevelt*
*American writer, conversationalist, politician, statesman,
who became the 25th president of the United States.*

"Never let the fear of striking out keep you from playing the game."
-Babe Ruth
A professional Baseball superstar who was talented in all aspects
of the sport, and one of the most celebrated athletes of all time.

"You have brains in your head.
You have feet in your shoes.
You can steer yourself any direction you choose."
-Dr. Seuss
A famous author for many children's book
using clever and creative wordplay.

"Whatever the mind of man can conceive and believe,
it can achieve."
-Napoleon Hill
American self-help author
who mostly promoted success in his writing.

"I would rather die of passion than of boredom."
-Vincent van Gogh
A dutch painter who became one of the most influential figures
in the history of Western Art.

"In the end, it's not the years in your life that count.
It's the life in your years."
-Abraham Lincoln
The 16th president of the United States,
who led the country during the American Civil War,
as well as pushing for the freedom of the slaves
within throughout the nation.

"Always remember that you are absolutely unique.
Just like everyone else."
-Margaret Mead
Anthropologist known for her adolescent studies.

Ruby is a Taiwanese Canadian who held a paint brush like a magic wand when she was a little girl. As she grew up, she decided to pursue studies in the realm of numbers. Being a mixture of creativity and reason, she often speaks in the abstract while expecting those around her to read her mind. One day, she decided to create stories from her own childhood encounters, stories that had their own messages. With elk being the spirit animal of wisdom, she wanted to spread the joy to future generations and help them discover the beauty of the world. How? Through the mind and writing of her partner in crime.

Sam is a Canadian from Hong Kong who always loved to doodle. He didn't settle for what his parents wanted him to do, instead followed his passion for art and design. Ruby reached out to him with the idea to spread knowledge to children with elk being the symbol. He had no clue what he was getting into, but he agreed anyway. He thought of the name that best suited the idea, Elkintales. From that point on, he became Ruby's partner in the journey to spread joy to future generations and help them discover the beauty of the world (do you have a clue what this means?), while trying to decipher his partner's encrypted mind.

You are unique.


You are special.


You are the best.

www.ingramcontent.com/pod-product-compliance
Lightning Source LLC
Chambersburg PA
CBHW040055240726
48664CB00004B/1200